Where I Live

POEMS ABOUT MY HOME, MY STREET, AND MY TOWN

selected by Paul B. Janeczko

illustrated by Hyewon Yum

CANDLEWICK PRESS

Contents

Home

Home . . . X.J. Kennedy 1

The Breakfast Boss . . . Janet Wong 2

The Window . . . Walter de la Mare 4

Our Rooftop . . . Amy Ludwig VanDerwater 5

Sunday Brunch . . . Reuben Jackson 6

Ode to a Sprinkler . . . Gary Soto 7

back yard . . . Valerie Worth 8

Crickets . . . Myra Cohn Livingston 9

The Train . . . Charlotte Zolotow 10

Our Cats . . . Wes Magee 11

Now the swing is still . . . Nicholas Virgilio 12

Street

Spruce Street, Berkeley . . . Naomi Shihab Nye 14

Sidewalk Cracks . . . Patricia Hubbell 15

Block Party . . . Nikki Grimes 16

Ode to My Shoes . . . Francisco X. Alarcón 17

Ice Cream Truck . . . Irene Latham 18

in yellow boots . . . Paul B. Janeczko 19

Over in the Pink House . . . Rebecca Kai Dotlich 20

The Tree on the Corner . . . Lilian Moore 21

October . . . Linda Sue Park 22

The Walk . . . Charles Waters 23

Snowplow . . . Hope Vestergaard 24

Town

If I Could Build a Town . . . Betsy Franco 26

People . . . Lois Lenski 27

Mrs. Peck-Pigeon . . . Eleanor Farjeon 28

At the Car Wash . . . Lin Oliver 29

Launderama . . . Iain Crichton Smith 30

Grocery Store Cat . . . Dave Crawley 31

New Kid at School . . . Betsy Franco 32

Recess . . . Avis Harley 33

Knoxville, Tennessee . . . Nikki Giovanni 34

Winter in the Park . . . Charles Ghigna 36

Snowy Benches . . . Aileen Fisher 37

City . . . Langston Hughes 38

Copyright Acknowledgments 40

Home

Home

East side, West side,
all around the town.
Which side
is the best side?
Wherever you sit down
to eat your supper, pet your cat,
do homework, watch TV.
Any old place
that's your home base
is where you want to be.

—X.J. Kennedy

The Breakfast Boss

Mom wakes me up
when she leaves for work.
It's my job
to wake my brothers up
an hour later.
I gently say their names
once, twice, and a third time.
I could yank their blankets off
to get them up fast
but I let them sleep
until the doorbell rings.
It's our neighbor Cristina
who is two years older than me
but two inches shorter.
She is The Breakfast Boss of us:
she makes sure we eat our cereal
while she peels the boiled eggs
Mom left in the pot.
We gulp our juice,
grab our homework,
and race to school
like bullet trains full of fuel—
ready to zoom ahead!

—Janet Wong

The Window

Behind the blinds I sit and watch
The people passing—passing by;
And not a single one can see
     My tiny watching eye.

They cannot see my little room,
All yellowed with the shaded sun;
They do not even know I'm here;
     Nor will guess when I am gone.

—Walter de la Mare

Our Rooftop

I go up there to be alone
to feel the wind play with my hair
to hear bright city sounds below
to breathe the periwinkle air
to read my latest chapter book
to nap on sweaty afternoons
to sit and draw or stand and think
to share my secrets with the moon.

A country kid might climb a tree
to see as far as he could see.
Our rooftop is the place for me—
the place where I feel free.

—Amy Ludwig VanDerwater

Sunday Brunch

and where
do your parents
summer?
she asked
him.

the front porch,
he replied.

—Reuben Jackson

Ode to a Sprinkler

There is no swimming
Pool on
Our street,
Only sprinklers
On lawns,
The helicopter
Of water
Slicing our legs.
We run through
The sprinkler,
Water on our
Lips, water
Dripping
From eyelashes,
Water like
Fat raindrops
That fall from
Skinny trees when
You're not looking.

—Gary Soto

back yard

Sun in the back yard
Grows lazy,

Dozing on the porch steps
All morning,

Getting up and nosing
About corners,

Gazing into an empty
Flowerpot,

Later easing over the grass
For a nap,

Unless
Someone hangs out the wash—

Which changes
Everything to a rush and a clap

Of wet
Cloth, and fresh wind

And sun
Wide awake in the white sheets.

—Valerie Worth

Crickets

they	tell
the	time
of	night
they	tick
the	time
of	night
they	tick
they	tell
of	night
they	tick
and	tell
the	time
they	tick
they	tell
the	time
they	click

—Myra Cohn Livingston

The Train

I hear it
home in my bed—
somewhere out in the night
the cry of a train
flying through
the darkness.
     To where?
     To whom?

—Charlotte Zolotow

Our Cats

Our cats stay out all night,
Moonlighting.
You should hear them spitting
And fighting!

At breakfast time they come in
Purring
And curl on chairs; no hint of
Stirring!

Then when it's dark they're off
Exploring
While thunder growls and gales
Are roaring!

When we're tucked-up in bed
Sound-sleeping
They're out there . . . in the darkness
. . . creeping!

—Wes Magee

Now the swing is still:
a suspended tire
        centers the autumn moon.

—Nicholas Virgilio

Street

Spruce Street, Berkeley

If a street is named for a tree,
it is right that flowers
bloom purple and feel like cats,
that people are leaves drifting
downhill in morning fog.

Everyone came outside to see
the moon setting like a perfect
orange mouth tipped up to heaven.

Now the cars sleep against curbs.
If I write a letter,
how will I make it long enough?

There is a place to stand
where you can see so many lights
you forget you are one of them.

—Naomi Shihab Nye

Sidewalk Cracks

Pavement cracks,
    sidewalk cracks,
        tracks, maps,
            charts to nowhere . . .
    everywhere . . .
somewhere . . .
        I followed a great long crooked crack
           past San Francisco
              once—
        a rough ten-blocker,
    west, around the Horn—
Guess I'll follow this one . . .
Who knows where?

—Patricia Hubbell

Block Party

Dear Danitra,

Tomorrow you're going to miss
those giant speakers
hissing and blasting
loud, fast music
into the crowded street.
There'll be no sense in my
trying to keep still.
You know how
that hot, hot dance beat
sizzles up through the concrete.
In a blink I become
a hip-swinging,
head-bopping,
foot-stomping,
fancy-dancying
fool.

—Nikki Grimes

Ode to My Shoes

my shoes
rest
all night
under my bed

tired
they stretch
and loosen
their laces

wide open
they fall asleep
and dream
of walking

they revisit
the places
they went to
during the day

and wake up
cheerful
relaxed
so soft

—Francisco X. Alarcón

Ice Cream Truck

On summer Mondays
    we listen

for the jinglesong
    that holds

half notes
    of winter:

fudgesicle
    orangesicle

pushpop
    bombpop

firecracker
    snowball

and ice cream
    on a stick

that drips
    unless

your tongue
    is swift
        like mine.

—Irene Latham

in yellow boots
the florist mists pails
of daffodils

her sidewalk the only one
with rainbows in the noon sun

—Paul B. Janeczko

Over in the Pink House

Over in the pink house,
over in the park,
lives a gang of kittens
meowing in the dark;
one is called Butter,
one is called Lump,
one is called Sugar,
jump,
jump,
jump.

—Rebecca Kai Dotlich

The Tree on the Corner

I've seen
the tree on the corner
in spring bud
and summer green.
Yesterday
it was yellow gold.

Then a cold
wind began to blow.
Now I know—
you really do not see
a tree
until you see
its bones.

—Lilian Moore

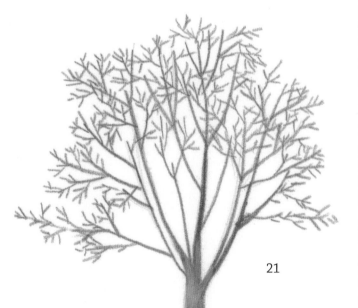

October

The wind rearranges the leaves,
as if to say, "Much better *there*,"
and coaxes others off their trees:
"It's lots more fun in the air."

Then it plays tag with a plastic bag,
and with one gust uncombs my hair!

—Linda Sue Park

The Walk

Crunching my boots
through another snowstorm,
each footprint a temporary tattoo
against the frosted prairie.

—Charles Waters

Snowplow

When everyone else
is tucked in bed
beneath a winter blanket,
the snowplow truck
has just begun
to push and scrape and bank it.
In blowing squalls
or sleety storms,
the snowplow's making piles
of slush and snow that line the streets
for miles and miles and miles.

—Hope Vestergaard

Town

TOYS

If I Could Build a Town

If I could build a town, well then,
I know just what I'd make:
an ice cream store, a toy shop,
and a store with bread and cake.

I guess I'd make a park
and build a nifty fire station.
Say, would you like to help me?
It just takes imagination!

—Betsy Franco

People

Tall people, short people,
Thin people, fat,
Lady so dainty
Wearing a hat,
Straight people, dumpy people,
Man dressed in brown;
Baby in a buggy—
These make a town.

—Lois Lenski

Mrs. Peck-Pigeon

Mrs. Peck-Pigeon
Is picking for bread,
Bob—bob—bob
Goes her little round head.
Tame as a pussy-cat
In the street,
Step—step—step
Go her little red feet.
With her little red feet
And her little round head,
Mrs. Peck-Pigeon
Goes picking for bread.

—Eleanor Farjeon

At the Car Wash

The vacuum sucks our cookie crumbs.
Next come the soapy suds.
Wash the windows, scrub the tires,
And lots of rub-a-dubs.

Rinse it clean with squirty water,
Dry it to a shine.
"Now, lookee there." My mommy smiles.
"Our car is mighty fine."

After dinner, in the bath,
With bubbles near and far,
I soap my arms and scrub my knees
Till I shine just like our car.

—Lin Oliver

Launderama

The clothes go bouncing up and down
the powder seethes and soaps
the load reverses and goes on
the light clicks off and stops.

The drier is as hot as fire
you fold your clothes away
cleaned of their rain and mud and mire
until another day.

—Iain Crichton Smith

Grocery Store Cat

He sits by himself
on the window shelf
in old Mister Galligan's store.
If you're passing by
and he catches your eye,
you can't help but walk through the door.

He purrs right on cue
as customers coo
and more and more visitors stop.
And once they're inside
they often decide:
"We may as well stay here and shop."

They pick up potatoes,
baked beans, and tomatoes,
while now and then pausing to chat.
As they walk down the aisles,
Mister Galligan smiles—
and winks at the grocery store cat.

—Dave Crawley

31

New Kid at School

Where did you come from?
Far away.
Miss your friends?
Every day.
Where do you live?
Maple Street.
What's your name?
Call me Pete.
How old are you?
Just turned eight.
You like hoops?
Yeah, great.
Got any friends?
Nope, not yet.
Wanna play?
You bet!

—Betsy Franco

Recess

Some play soccer,
Some run races,
Others read
In quiet places.

Some find leaves
Or draw with chalk,
Some play tag
While others talk.

A few play chess,
Lots play ball,
And some just like
To watch it all.

—Avis Harley

Knoxville, Tennessee

I always like summer
best
you can eat fresh corn
from daddy's garden
and okra
and greens
and cabbage
and lots of
barbecue
and buttermilk
and homemade ice-cream
at the church picnic
and listen to
gospel music
outside
at the church
homecoming
and go to the mountains with
your grandmother
and go barefooted
and be warm
all the time
not only when you go to bed
and sleep

—Nikki Giovanni

Winter in the Park

Last night an ice storm came to town
And dressed the fountain in a gown.

Icicles hung from the trees
Like chandeliers out in the breeze.

Each statue wore a fancy dress,
A frozen garment for each guest.

A night of magic in the dark,
A winter ballroom in the park.

—Charles Ghigna

Snowy Benches

Do parks get lonely
in winter, perhaps,
when benches have only
snow on their laps?

—Aileen Fisher

City

In the morning the city
Spreads its wings
Making a song
In stone that sings.

In the evening the city
Goes to bed
Hanging lights
About its head.

—Langston Hughes

Copyright Acknowledgments

For my mother
HY

Compilation copyright © 2023 by Paul B. Janeczko
Illustrations copyright © 2023 by Hyewon Yum
Copyright acknowledgments appear on pages 40–41.

First edition 2023

Library of Congress Catalog Card Number 2022908176
ISBN 978-1-5362-0094-2

22 23 24 25 26 27 CCP 10 9 8 7 6 5 4 3 2 1

Printed in Shenzhen, Guangdong, China

This book was typeset in Chaparral Pro.
The illustrations were done in colored pencil and watercolor.

Candlewick Press
99 Dover Street
Somerville, Massachusetts 02144

www.candlewick.com